Hopping

Michael Catchpool

illustrated by David Roberts

MARKS &
SPENCER

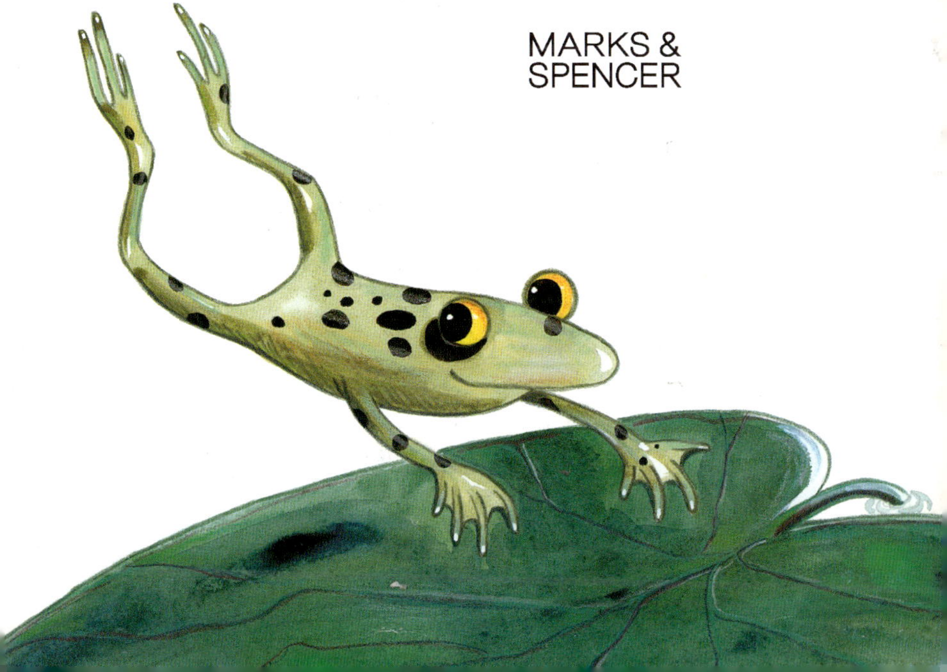

Fred lived next door to Finn.
Fred had five frogs and so did Finn.

One night when the moon was up and the grass was damp, Finn's five frogs called to Fred's frogs, "Come on over, we're having a party!"

"What an excellent idea!" Fred's frogs croaked back. "We'll be right over!" And they hopped over the fence.

The frogs dived and splashed and flipped and flopped and had a fantastic time.

By the time the sun was coming up they could hardly manage a hop.

"Phew!" croaked Fred's frogs. "We really must be getting home," and they dragged themselves back over the fence.

The next morning, as the sun sparkled on the water, Fred stood idly counting his frogs.

"One, two, three, FOUR!"

Then he looked over the fence
and counted the frogs in Finn's pond.
"One, two, three, four, five, SIX!"
Fred was furious.

"Frog thief!" he shouted at Finn. "You should have five frogs and you've got six. You've stolen one of mine!" And Fred marched into Finn's garden and snatched a frog before Finn could say a word.

"I'll soon put an end to your stealing!" shouted Fred, and with some wood and some nails he built his fence higher and higher.

That evening, as an owl swooped across the sky, Fred's five frogs called to Finn's five frogs, "Come over to our pond tonight for some fun."

"What an excellent idea!" croaked Finn's frogs.

The frogs frolicked and feasted on flies until they were completely exhausted.

"Time to be getting home," they croaked.

Then Finn's frogs squeezed back under the fence.

The next day, as the birds were singing in the trees, Finn slowly counted his frogs, "One, two, THREE!"

He glared over the fence into Fred's pond. "One, two, three, four, five, six, SEVEN!"

Finn was fuming. "Frog thief!" he shouted at Fred. "You have seven frogs and I've only got three."

He marched right round to Fred's garden and snatched back his two frogs.

"I'll stop you pinching my frogs!" said Finn, and he dug a big, wide ditch by the fence.

That evening, Finn's five frogs called to Fred's, "Why not party in our pond tonight?"

So Fred's frogs scrambled over the huge fence and leaped over the enormous ditch.

The frogs had a splendid time, diving and swimming, dancing and singing until they could hardly croak.

Just before dawn, Fred's frogs returned home. They leaped back over the enormous ditch and scrambled back over the huge fence.

The following morning, while the dew glistened on the grass, Fred carefully counted his frogs.

"One, TWO!"

Then he counted the frogs in Finn's pond.

"One, two, three, four, five, six, seven, EIGHT!"

Fred was frantic.

“Frog thief!” he shouted at Finn. “You’ve stolen three of my frogs,” and he marched through the gate and snatched back his frogs. “I’ll put a stop to this,” Fred said, and he put a great big cage right over his frogs and his pond.

That evening, Fred's five frogs called to Finn's frogs. "We can't play tonight, we've been locked up."

"Then we'll come over to you," croaked Finn's frogs, and they leaped across the great big ditch, over the high fence and opened the door of the cage.

"Phew!" said Fred's frogs. "You know, us frogs need our freedom," and off they hopped, with Finn's frogs close behind.

Now Fred has no frogs.
And neither does Finn.